Julia

Death Valley's Youngest Victim

The Heroic Rescue
of the
Stranded 1849ers

Cover photo by LeRoy Johnson
Telescope Peak from the emigrants' trail near the west
side road, Death Valley

FOREWORD

Sketches and quotes not otherwise cited are from the first edition of *Death Valley in '49* by William Lewis Manly, 1894. Manly consistently spelled *Arcan* as Arcane, but *Arcan* is the spelling used on the family tombstones. The name has also been spelled Arcain, indicating a long "a" pronunciation. We use Arcan throughout.

We express our sincerest appreciation to Matt* and Rosemary* Ryan, Mary* and Paul DeDecker, and Ardis* and Gayle* Walker who have been particularly valuable as guides and mentors for our Death Valley research. Pete Sanchez and other Death Valley National Monument staff also have been very helpful. We thank The Bancroft and Huntington Libraries for access to original '49er documents.

FOREWORD TO SECOND EDITION

Between 1981 and 1986 we finished our research on the camps along the Bennett-Arcan families' escape route from Death Valley and came to a few conclusions that differ from those in the first edition. In 1987, the University of Nevada Press published our book *Escape from Death Valley,* which provides extensive footnotes and presents, for the first time since 1888, the Death Valley portion of Manly's first published account called "From Vermont to California."

In this edition of *Julia* we have added maps, notes, an index, additional background, and an auto log for those who wish to follow the route by car. We appreciate the help given us by Renie Leaman, President of HELP (Help Evergreen [Cemetery] Live Permanently) and Hal Rommel* of Santa Cruz, California, in our search for background on the Arcan family.

Quotations not referenced are from the first edition of William Lewis Manly's book *Death Valley in '49.*

* Deceased

JULIA

DEATH VALLEY'S YOUNGEST VICTIM

In a fog-shrouded cemetery surrounded by redwoods towering into the mist, we searched for the gravestones of the Arcan family. The mossy marble slabs, the distant crashing of ocean surf, the damp, green grass of the oldest cemetery in Santa Cruz, California, were a vivid contrast to the stark and glaring deserts of Southern California where we carried out most of our field research on the gold-seekers of 1849.

Our interest centered on the Arcan and Bennett families, emigrants who struggled through Death Valley on their perilous trek across the continent in search of California's Mother Lode. The Arcan family—John Baptiste, his wife Abigail, and their 2-year-old son Charley—were one of the two families who, among the 100 or so argonauts, forged a tortuous trail through the Great American Desert in the winter of 1849-50 in search of a shortcut from the Old Spanish Trail in Utah to Walker Pass in the southern Sierra Nevada.

These emigrants hoped to cut 500 miles off the long, desolate trail that wound from Salt Lake City southward to the Pueblo de Los Angeles and north to the gold fields. Little did they suspect that the shortcut would end in the loss of most of their worldly possessions and death for four of them. The Arcan and Bennett families were stranded in, and heroically rescued from, the very heart of that treacherous desert—Death Valley.

At last we found the Arcan burial plot in Evergreen Cemetery where John's gravestone stood guard over his final resting place. While LeRoy attempted to take photographs in the mist, Jean read a small sign attached to a slender metal rod stuck in the ground near John's gravestone.

Suddenly she blurted out, "Good heavens! Mrs. Arcan was five months pregnant when she walked the 250 miles out of Death Valley to the Rancho San Francisco. Listen to this!"

JULIA ARCAN

Julia is the oldest recorded death in Evergreen. She died at the age of 19 days in July, 1850. Her family was with the Manly, Wade & Bennett parties' wagon train that became marooned in Death Valley in December 1849 while looking for a shortcut to the gold fields. Mr. Manly eventually went for, and returned with help the beginning of February. Julia was born the following July. Her headstone disappeared two years ago. When last seen it was broken in half and measured about 14 inches wide by 22 inches long. The following poem was carved on it——

A little time on earth she spent

'Till God for her his angel sent

And then on time she closed her eyes

To wake in glory in the skies.

The space between the graves of John Baptiste and Julia Arcan is probably Abigail's final resting place, but there is no stone or other record of her burial.

The two pieces of Julia Arcan's tombstone, for a while misplaced, are finally returned to her grave in Evergreen Cemetery, Santa Cruz, California.

What a shock!   In all the years we had researched the Death Valley '49ers we had no indication Abigail was pregnant. Throughout the hundreds of pages written by William Lewis Manly in his two accounts, "From Vermont to California" and *Death Valley in '49*,[1] and in the accounts of

---

[1] Manly's "From Vermont to California" is found in: LeRoy and Jean Johnson, *Escape from Death Valley* (Nevada Press, 1987, U of NV Reno). William Lewis Manly's *Death Valley in '49* is photographically reproduced by Community Press, Bishop, CA, 1977. Hayday Press, Berkeley,

8 ~†~

others who traveled through Death Valley, there was no hint of Abigail's condition—or was there?

We left the graveyard deeply moved by the discovery of baby Julia's brief life and puzzled by the apparent theft of an infant's tombstone.

That evening we reread parts of Manly's accounts to see if we had overlooked some hint of Abigail's condition, and yes, there were faint clues. Manly remarked that Abigail did not run out with the others to greet him when he and John Rogers returned with provisions for the two families waiting in Death Valley, and she and John sat apart from the others as preparations were made for the journey out of the desert. Her reticence may have been due to her pregnancy.

The condition of pregnancy and the momentous occasion of childbirth were rarely chronicled in the mid-1800s. Diaries from the western migration, including those written by women, mention pregnancy only obliquely: "Mrs. Lamore, suddenly sickened and died.... We halted a day to bury her and the infant that had lived but an hour." Another diarist said, "There was a woman died in this train yesterday. She left six children, one of them only two days old." Another emigrant woman recalled, "Three days after my little sister Lettie drank the laudanum and died we stopped for a few hours, and my sister Olivia was born. We were so late that the men of the party decided we could not tarry a day, so we had to press on."[2] In reference to a letter written by Phoebe Stanton in 1847, Kenneth Holmes wrote the following, "There is one fact that does not appear in Phoebe Stanton's letters, but it can be deduced by historical detection: She was pregnant during the long westward journey, for the 1850 Federal

CA, 2001, has published the newest edition of Manly's book with our footnotes, epilogue, and index.

[2] Lillian Schlissel, *Women's Diaries of the Westward Journey* (Schocken Books, 1982, New York:), pp. 51, 183, & 223.

Census lists a little boy, Philip, three years old, born in Oregon."[3] Mr. Holmes presents similar examples throughout succeeding volumes of his compilation of women's diaries. It seems strange today that pregnancy and childbirth were once thought to be an embarrassment too great to be mentioned.

The physical and emotional complications that pregnant emigrant women endured added to their burden of caring for sick or injured children, tending to household chores in primitive conditions, and taking on a husband's duties when he became ill or died. The lack of water, bending over a smoking camp fire, walking along the dusty trail to spare the oxen, packing and unpacking the wagon, all the chores of trail life were made worse by the condition of pregnancy. The travails these stoic women experienced gave them a far different outlook on the journey than that of their male traveling companions. As Lillian Schlissel said of pioneer women, "The decision to make the journey rested with the men, and farm men of the early nineteenth century were not inclined to excuse women from their daily responsibilities to prepare for the occasion of childbirth. Women were expected to be strong enough to serve the common needs of the day, and strong enough to meet the uncommon demands as well. The society of emigrants yielded little comfort to frailty or timidity—or, for that matter, to motherhood."[4]

Later we discovered that Julia's headstone had not been stolen, just quietly put away for safe keeping. Stan Kloth, a member of the current organization of Death Valley '49ers, told us how it happened: "I worked for the city of Santa Cruz Park Department and the park I took care of

---

[3] Kenneth Holmes, ed. & comp. *Covered Wagon Women: Diaries & Letters from the Western Trails 1840-1890*, Vol. I (Arthur Clark Co., 1983, Glendale. CA), p. 84.

[4] Lillian Schlissel, p. 35. (*See note 2.*)

borders the cemetery and I was trying to help stop the vandals in the cemetery by picking up the broken headstones and storing them."[5] Later Hal Rommel tracked down the broken stone and deposited it in the attic of the Santa Cruz City Museum where we found it. Thanks to HELP (Help Evergreen Live Permanently), it is now repaired and returned to Evergreen Cemetery where it covers Julia's final resting place near that of her father.

History has recorded only one death as occurring in Death Valley that is attributable to the sufferings of the '49ers, an older man named Captain Culverwell. But in our opinion, Julia Arcan's death also can be attributed to her short stay in the valley called Death—and to her mother's desperate escape from it. Julia spent two of her most formative months, the months before she was born, in Death Valley where her mother suffered near-starvation conditions.

The saga of how Julia's family struggled into Death Valley and how they were rescued from certain death in its confines is one of the West's great heroic adventure stories. Julia's death after her mother's desperate struggle to survive the desert ordeal adds a poignant aftermath to this amazing story.

John (Jean) Baptiste Arcan, Julia's father, was born in Versailles, France, in 1813 and immigrated to Quebec with his parents. At some point, he moved to New York where he mastered the trades of brush maker, carpenter, and gunsmith before moving west. He married Abigail Harriet Ericsen of Massachusetts, and in Chicago on May 1, 1848, their son Charley was born. The family headed for California in the spring of 1849, and by September they had traveled as far as the Mormon settlement beside the Great Salt Lake. They were fortunate to arrive

5 Stan Kloth, letter to authors, Sept. 17, 1979.

with both their wagons and the two teamsters who helped drive them.

With winter approaching, the emigrants were reminded of the horrible fate of the Donner party in the Sierra Nevada two years before and the report of Fremont's disastrous 4th expedition in the Colorado mountains the previous winter. Many of the emigrants in Salt Lake City were convinced they should not attempt a Sierra Nevada crossing with the approach of winter. Gradually, a large wagon train assembled to attempt the long and circuitous southern route to the gold fields. Captain Jefferson Hunt, a Mormon elder who was familiar with the new southern route, was hired to lead about 100 wagons over part of the Old Spanish Trail to the Pueblo de Los Angeles. He warned the emigrants that some of their cattle would die along the trail since feed was sparse and water holes were far apart. The wagons congregated at Hobble Creek south of what is now Provo, Utah, to wait for the cooler weather of the fall season. On October 2, 1849, the train began its long southern trek.

As was true with many wagon trains heading to the California gold fields, disagreement developed over leadership of the train and about the route to be taken. When some men passing by on horseback displayed a map showing water and grass along a shorter, western route, most of the emigrants turned their wagons west with the hope of cutting time and distance from their journey.

The hand-drawn map, apparently sketched by a mountain man by the name of Barney Ward, was reinforced by John Fremont's famous map published in 1848. Fremont's map showed a mountain range stretching east to west across the blank part of the Great Basin with the words, "DIVIDING RANGE BETWEEN THE WATERS OF THE PACIFIC AND THE WATERS OF THE GREAT BASIN." If such a mountain range existed, surely water and grass could be found along its base. The emigrants threw caution aside and ignored

Fremont's dire warning: "These mountains are not explored, being only seen from elevated points on the northern exploring line." They disregarded the word "U n e x p l o r e d" printed in large letters across the suspiciously blank section of his map.

On November 4, all but six wagons left Captain Hunt's leadership and turned west in a foolhardy attempt to save time and distance. By this time Abigail Arcan was about one month pregnant with Julia, and she probably began to suspect her condition.

When the defectors came to a seemingly impassable barrier, now called Beaver Dam Wash west of Cedar City, Utah, many of them wisely returned to Captain Hunt's trail and followed him into Southern California where they arrived in Los Angeles seven weeks later with little mishap.

The remaining 85 or so men, four women, and eleven children who took the so-called shortcut, relied on their pioneering spirit as they struck west into the unknown. Little did they suspect that months of hardship, privation, and death awaited them.

There was little cohesion among those who took the short cut. Separate groups of men labeled themselves by such names as the Jayhawkers, the Mississippi Boys, and the Bug Smashers. Other groups were created when solitary men banded together in their mutual desire to reach the gold fields. The strong-willed and vocal Reverend James W. Brier, with his petite wife Juliet, and their three young boys—Columbus, John, and Kirk—insisted upon traveling close on the heels of these male groups even though the men had voted against accepting family groups as traveling companions.

The Arcans traveled with the Bennett family: Asabel, his wife Sarah, and their three young children under age ten—George, Melissa, and little Martha, who was just old enough to climb in and out of the wagons. Traveling with the Bennett family were William Lewis Manly, Asabel's part-time hunting companion from southwestern Wisconsin; Manly's wagon-train and Green River-venturing friend, John Haney Rogers; and two teamsters who drove Bennett's two wagons. As time passed, other wagons joined the small Bennett-Arcan train until there were about seven wagons traveling together. Since Manly did not have to drive a wagon, he took the responsibility of scouting ahead in search of water and the best route.

The Wade family traveled a day behind the Bennett-Arcan train. Henry Wade, Mary, their four children—George, Charles, Almira, and Richard—and possibly a driver for their second wagon made up their party. By trailing the others by a day, the Wades had the advantage of a road to follow and exclusive use of the springs Manly had discovered.

Travel along the "shortcut" was particularly difficult for Juliet Brier (called Julia by her friends) and for Mary Wade who did not have the companionship of other women during the months of hardship they faced in the desert. Lack of privacy in the open desert and a shortage of water for cleanliness were particularly vexing privations. Abigail Arcan and Sarah Bennett were fortunate to have one another's company.

As the small caravans toiled around the corrugations of short, north-south mountain ranges in central Nevada, the emigrants realized Fremont's east-west mountain range was imaginary and based on speculation. Without the grass and good water they had expected to find, the oxen grew weak, and provisions ran low. In western Nevada the Brier family and the Georgia-Mississippi boys were forced to abandon their wagons when the oxen could no longer pull them. One night someone stole meat from the Bennett's cooking pot, and the families were put on short rations. For everyone, water became more valuable than gold. The Jayhawkers suffered from lack of water for five days straight before they were saved by an

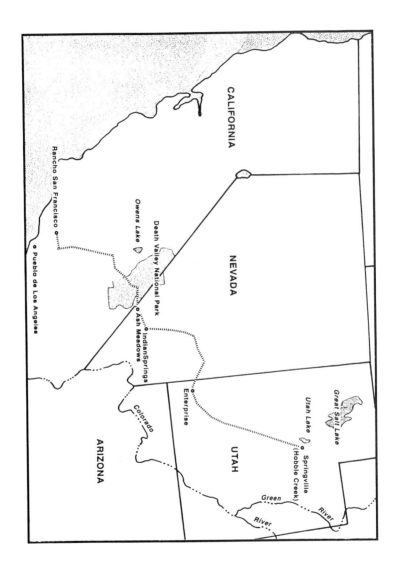

Route of the Bennett-Arcan Party from Hobble Creek, Utah, to the Rancho San Francisco near Saugus, in southern California.

unexpected snowstorm that fell like manna from heaven. Manly said of the Bennett-Arcan party:

> The four children were crying for water but there was not a drop to give them.... The mothers were nearly crazy, for they expected the children would choke with thirst and die in their arms.... They reproached themselves as being the cause of all this trouble. For the love of gold they had left homes where hunger had never come.[6]

On Christmas Eve, 1849, Bennett and Arcan's four, travel-scarred wagons stood near a flickering campfire on the desolate alluvial fan northwest of today's Death Valley Junction. Loneliness, anxiety, memories of good homes left behind, and prayers for deliverance from the desert were in the minds and hearts of the two families as they made yet another camp along this interminable "shortcut" to the gold fields. The Earhart and Schlögel wagons stood nearby; the Wade family wagons were a day behind. Louis Nusbaumer and his companions Hadapp, Fish, Culverwell, Isham, and Smith were camped a short distance away. Nusbaumer wrote in his journal:

> Our prospects begin to become more dismal again since one of our oxen is about to die, though we will not lose courage on the eve of the day on which our Savior was born.... Christmas in the mountains of California.... This day was in general a day of sorrow for us, since the previously mentioned ox was no longer in a condition to go on and we were forced to throw away all our possessions in order to lighten the wagon enough that 1 yoke of oxen can pull it.[7]

About 22 miles to the west, the Brier family and the Mississippi boys were camped at Travertine Springs among the barren hills in Furnace Creek Wash overlooking the deep depression now called Death Valley. They prepared the only

---

[6] Quotes not referenced are from Manly's book *Death Valley in '49.*

[7] Louis Nusbaumer's diary in *Escape From Death Valley,* pp. 160-168. *(See note 1.)*

Christmas feast available to them: "An ox was butchered," Mrs. Brier recalled, "and having some bread with plenty of coffee we feasted and rested.... They called Mr. B[rier] Parson. Toward evening one came to him and said, Parson we would like to have you give us a lecture this evening. He complied and gave them one on Education." Since the Briers had abandoned their wagons a few days before, they had crossed the Funeral Mountains on foot and worked their way down Furnace Creek Wash. Mrs. Brier spoke of her difficult trek:

> Night came and no water. All day long I had walked in silence, not in sight or hearing of a soul except my little ones. There was no moon and the stars shone faintly. My little 4 year old boy gave out.... Taking him on my back—[I] carried him until my breath almost left me ... time after time I carried him. The ground was hard, composed of small pieces of broken rock and the feet of the oxen made but little impression and I sometimes was obliged to get down and hunt for the track.... Suddenly we came round the point of a high rock, a fire was burning and Mr. Brier was setting by it. I said is this the camp. He answered No. They have found water six miles ahead.[8]

For two days the Bennett and Arcan families labored over the Funeral Mountains and rolled into Travertine Springs two days after Christmas. By this time the Briers, Jayhawkers, and Georgia-Mississippi Boys had moved north into Death Valley.

While the Bennett and Arcan families rested near the warm waters of Travertine Springs, Manly walked seventeen miles north to visit the Jayhawkers' camp at McLean Spring, the head-water of Salt Creek. He found them dismantling their wagons and burning the dry oak planks to smoke the meat from their emaciated oxen. They

---

8 Juliet Brier, letter to Jayhawker reunion, Jan. 1905, JA 106, Jayhawker Collection, Huntington Library, San Marino, CA.

were abandoning their worldly possessions and preparing for a final desperate march to the gold fields. They prayed that only one mountain range remained to be crossed, but instead, they were destined to find five more ranges—the Panamint, Slate, Argus, El Paso, and San Gabriel ranges each separated by barren deserts.

While Manly was investigating the Jayhawkers' northern route, Indians shot arrows into the Bennett-Arcan oxen in Furnace Creek Wash, which the white men interpreted as an attack of retribution for the squashes the party had taken from an Indian encampment a few days before. But such was not the case. The Death Valley Indians, whose winter camp was at the mouth of Furnace Creek Wash where the Inn now stands, knew nothing of the Nevada depredation, but they did know food when they saw it. The attack was not against the immigrants; rather it was an attempt to procure fresh meat. The desert Indians were often on the verge of starvation since they depended in large part on the inconsistent mesquite bean and pinyon nut crops.

Most of the grass around Travertine Springs had been eaten by the Jayhawker and Brier oxen; as more cattle arrived, pulling the Wade, Earhart, and Schlögel wagons, the Bennetts and Arcans decided to move on. They could not get their four wagons out of the valley by going north, and nothing could be gained by retracing their steps to the east. Nor could they cross the towering, snow covered Panamint Range to the west. Only by going south could they hope to get their wagons out of the desert.

The two families followed an Indian trail southward and across Death Valley as it led over the northern fringe of Devil's Golf Course near the current road crossing. Turning south on the west side of the salt pan they traveled the smooth margin between the salty lake deposits and the rough, boulder-strewn alluvial fans. One night they camped beside the fresh water at Eagle

Borax Spring (called Emigrant Spring on some early maps). By this time, Bennett and Arcan's four teamsters had decided to cast their lot with the other single men. They abandoned the families on the west side of Death Valley and struck north to follow the Jayhawkers.[9]

There were numerous signs of Indian habitation along the trail—wickiups, sleeping circles, food caches, and burial mounds. Cuff, Bennett's faithful yellow mastiff, kept watch for Indians while always on the lookout for small rodents to eat. Some of these Indian rock circles are still visible along the twenty-mule team and old auto road that parallels the existing westside road.

The next day, in a grove of mesquite trees among some sand hills, they came to a "mound about four feet high and in the top of this a little well that held about a pailful of water that was quite strong of sulphur," as Manly described it. Today, this water hole has dried up without leaving a trace. However, based on Manly's description, we've determined it was at or near the site of Mesquite Well located about seven and a half miles south of Bennetts Well. This was the southern-most potable water found in Death Valley and was later used by the twenty-mule teams as their final camp before crossing Wingate Wash and on to Daggett or Mojave.[10]

From the sulphur water well, the Bennett and Arcan families attempted to cross the Panamint Range with their wagons, but they had to turn back when the weakened oxen could not conquer

[9] The spring was renamed Eagle Borax when Isadore Daunet established the Eagle Borax Works there in 1882. Rows of borax mounds can still be seen on the flats east of the spring.

[10] LeRoy and Jean Johnson, "The Bennett-Arcan Long Camp and Manly's Sulphur Water Well" (Proceedings: Death Valley Conference on History and Prehistory, 1987), pp. 22-43.

the steep grade leading to Warm Spring Canyon. They retreated to the little well where they found the Wade family and the remainder of the small train encamped. That night the men discussed and argued about where they were in relation to the gold fields. Some thought the snowy mountain range towering above their heads must be the mighty Sierra Nevada. Others thought it was the Coast Mountains shown on Fremont's map. If the latter were true, the Pueblo de Los Angeles was not far away.

Bennett suggested that Manly and Rogers hike across the mountain and bring back horses for the women and children to ride and food for all those remaining in Death Valley. The "boys," as Asabel Bennett called Manly and Rogers, were expected to make the round trip easily in two weeks.[11]

After the boys left, those remaining in Death Valley returned to the more plentiful water at what is now called Eagle Borax Spring. Their food supply was badly depleted, and malnutrition was already taking its merciless toll. Nusbaumer and Hadapp were suffering from serious swelling in their lower limbs—symptoms of scurvy. And what of Abigail and her unborn child? Their plight was equally serious.

The Wade family decided to push south and not wait for Manly and Rogers to return with provisions and horses. Very soon, the Earharts, Nusbaumer, Hadapp, Culverwell, Schlögel, indeed all the other men, followed the Wades southward, and ultimately crossed Cajon Pass into the Los

---

[11] In "From Vermont to California," Manly said "a week or ten days," but in his book he said fifteen days. After surveying the country from Manly Lookout 11 miles south of Telescope Peak, Manly said, "we could not reach a settlement and return in one week nor in twenty days either." In *Escape from Death Valley*, p. 71.

Angeles basin. The Bennett and Arcan families were left stranded in Death Valley.[12]

When Manly and Rogers reached the backbone of the Panamint Range, they were devastated to discover the Sierra Nevada was still 60 miles to the west and the Coast Range barely visible in the shimmering haze to the south. The boys realized they could never cover the vast distance to obtain supplies and return within the allotted two weeks, but neither could they return empty-handed to the starving families waiting for them, so onward they boldly trudged.

During their harrowing trek of 250 miles, they passed the body of Mr. Fish on the eastern slope of Manly Pass in the Slate Range. Later they learned from the Jayhawkers that William Isham, Mr. Fish's traveling companion, had died a day later after crawling through the yielding sands of Searles Valley. Previously both men had been traveling with the Bennett-Arcan train but had left it at Travertine Springs to follow the Jayhawkers who exited Death Valley via Towne Pass.

Manly and Rogers hiked west to the base of the Sierra Nevada, nearly dying from lack of water. When they discovered that snow storms had closed Walker Pass, they were forced to continue south and across the Mojave Desert before reaching the San Gabriel Mountains— Fremont's "Coast Mountains."

After crossing the mountains through Soledad Pass, also covered with snow, and making their way slowly through the thick brush in Soledad Canyon, they came at last to civilization—the Rancho San Francisco—where they received help.

The Rancho was a huge tract of land now occupied by the towns of Saugus and Newhall at the foot of Soledad Canyon. The ranch house had been an *asistencia*, or outlying boarding house, of

---

[12] The Wades were the only Death Valley '49ers to succeed in bringing a wagon through to Los Angeles.

Mission San Fernando, but by 1849, it was turned over to private ownership and was occupied by the Del Valle family. Here Manly and Rogers obtained two horses as well as beans, corn, and wheat; the latter two they ground into course flour to take back to those awaiting them in Death Valley.[13] On their return to Death Valley, they chanced upon some road builders in San Francisquito Canyon from whom they bought flour, a white mare, and a little one-eyed mule.

Manly and Rogers rushed back to Death Valley as fast as the horses and their own feet would carry them. The horses died on the way—they could not eat the brush nor drink the salty water—but the little mule came through after performing acrobatic feats along a precipitous cliff skirting a dry waterfall while crossing the Panamint Range. The boys arrived at the sulphur water hole twenty-five days after they left, foot sore and anxious about the families. They were already two weeks late and feared the families had attempted to leave the valley without their guidance. The next day, on the final leg of their perilous trek, the boys found the body of Captain Culverwell sprawled on the desert sand. They were now more fearful than ever about the fate of the families. Soon they saw the wagons with the canvas covers torn off, and Manly later described the desolate scene.

> One hundred yards now to the wagons and still no sign of life, no positive sign of death, though we looked carefully for both. We fear that perhaps there are Indians in ambush ... I fired the shot. Still as death and not a move for a moment, and then as if by magic a man came out from under a wagon and stood up looking all around, for he did

---

[13] The California Historical Landmark at Castaic Junction commemorates the site of the ranch house, which is one-half mile south on a small hill. Rancho San Francisco was mistakenly called Rancho San Francisquito by Manly and other Death Valley '49ers probably because a nearby canyon was named San Francisquito Canyon.

not see us. Then he threw up his arms high over his head and shouted—"The boys have come! The boys have come!"

John Arcan, Asabel and Sarah Bennett, and Cuff ran out to meet them. Abigail, now over four months pregnant, remained in the shade under a wagon.

The families were no longer camped at Eagle Borax Spring; they had moved two and a half miles southward to take advantage of fresh grass and better water at a site later called Bennetts Well. They were preparing their escape from the valley, fearful that Indians had surely killed Manly and Rogers.[14] The two young men related their adventures while preparations for the exodus continued. Manly and Sarah made breast straps and breeching for the oxen as they talked in the shade of one wagon while the Arcans worked nearby listening to every word of the ordeal that lay ahead.

Little Martha Bennett, about two years old, had been seriously ill while the boys were traveling. Because Martha and little Charley Arcan were unable to walk, pouches were made from two hickory shirts to carry them on either side of Old Crump, the trustworthy brindle ox with a bent horn. George and Melissa were old enough to ride on his back.

After preparations were completed for the long journey out of the desert, the little caravan started southward from Bennetts Well. There were eleven thin oxen; one carried two kegs of water, Old Crump carried the four children, Abigail and Sarah each rode an ox, and the rest packed small parcels of baggage. The little one-eyed mule was entrusted with the valuable beans

[14] LeRoy and Jean Johnson, "The Bennett-Arcan Long Camp and Manly's Sulphur Water Well" (Proceedings: Death Valley Conference on History and Prehistory, 1987), pp. 22-43.

and flour, and Cuff kept an eye out for Indians and potential morsels of food.

Abigail refused to leave behind "some articles of finery, of considerable value and much prized." Among these was a treasured tablecloth she had made that she tied about her waist. She put on her best dress and decorated her finest hat with bright ribbons leaving the ends long to flutter in the wind saying she would not "leave them here to deck the red man's wife, and have her go flirting over the mountains."

After the little caravan had traveled about four miles, a pack slid to the underside of one of the oxen, and he began to buck. His terror was contagious; "with elevated tails and terrible plunges [they] would kick and thrash and run till the packs came off." The babies were pulled from their pockets as George, Melissa, and Sarah Bennett jumped to safety. But not Abigail Arcan.

> Mrs. Arcane proved to be a good rider, and hard to unseat, clinging desperately to her strap as she was tossed up and down, and whirled about at a rate enough to make any one dizzy. Her many fine ribbons flew out behind like the streamers from a mast-head, and the many fancy fixin's she had donned fluttered in the air in gayest mockery. Eventually she was thrown however, but without the least injury to herself.

Such a ride would have taxed an experienced rodeo rider not to mention a pregnant woman.

They made camp at once to repair the damage. After confirming that Abigail was all right and sharing in a hearty laugh, John Arcan returned to Bennetts Well to replenish the water that spilled from the kegs. John Rogers and Asabel Bennett continued down the trail a mile or so to bury Captain Culverwell's body. He had left the Bennett-Arcan camp with the other men about two weeks before the boys returned, but being unable to keep up with the others, he attempted to return to the families only to die alone and uncomforted on the sandy trail.

The oxen get frisky. Manly wrote T. S. Palmer saying, "I never tried before to make a picture on paper until I made up my mind to show my friends the sunken valley so much talked of and written about. The sketches in my book are only to show the reader how we worked our way from purgatory to heaven. Manly made sketches for an artist to use to make3 illustrations in his book Death Valley in `49.

The most strenuous days of Abigail's life were about to begin. She had to walk 250 miles over jagged rocks, through deep sand, around sage-brush and cactus wearing no boots or shoes, with only the hide of a freshly slaughtered ox to protect her feet. She had to climb mountains and cross deserts, and she must not slow the march or the lives of her friends and family would be in jeopardy. She would have very little water and only one meal served after she stumbled into camp after dark each night.

Instead of continuing south to the little sulfur water well, Asabel decided they should "take a nearer route to the summit, so as to more quickly reach the water holes" at Arrastre Spring above Butte Valley. From the floor of Death Valley, the families had to ascend the mountain to an elevation of 5,790 feet in a distance of about 16 miles. It was impossible to make the distance and steep ascent in one day, so they were forced to camp part way up the eastern flank of the Panamint Range, either in the south fork of Six Springs Canyon or in Galena Canyon.

> Mrs. Arcane said her limbs ached so much she did not think she could even go on the next day. They had climbed over the rocks all day, and were lame and sore, and truly thought they could not endure such another day. The trail had been more like stairs than a road in its steep ascent.... The women did not recover sufficient energy to remove their clothing, but slept as they were, and sat up and looked around with uncombed hair in the morning, perfect pictures of dejection ... their swollen eyes and stiffened joints told how sadly unprepared they were to go forward at once.

The next day they reached Arrastre Spring, and while they were encamped there, the women rested in camp and John Rogers herded the oxen as Asabel Bennett, John Arcan, and Manly climbed to the crest of the Panamints to survey the route ahead. As they returned to camp, they looked into the hazy depths of the valley where they had buried Captain Culverwell, and as they

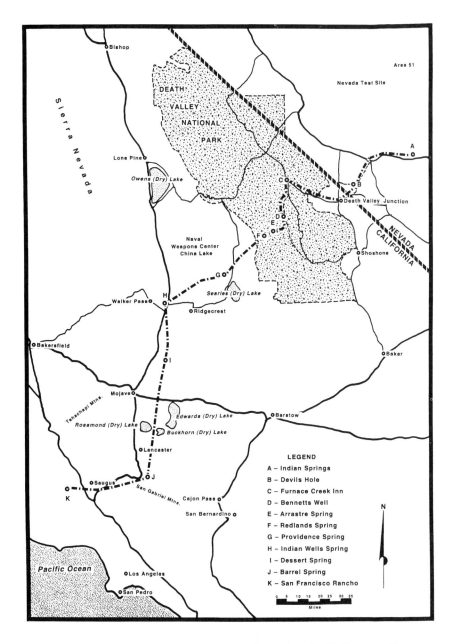

The Bennett-Arcan escape route from Death Valley to the Rancho San Francisco. The letters refer to sites described in the travel log at the end of this book.

doffed their hats one of them intoned, *"Good bye Death Valley."*[15]

Meanwhile, John Rogers watched the oxen as they fed on the bunch grass in Butte Valley and the women rested near the spring in sight of the many Indian signs that surrounded this important water hole. The next day, the bedraggled party skirted the western edge of Butte Valley and descended Redlands Canyon to its spring.

When the company arrived at the first dry fall below the spring, the same fall Manly and Rogers had difficulty getting the little mule around on their return trip to Death Valley, the men feared they could not get the oxen down it alive. Without their food on the hoof, so to speak, the families might starve. So the men piled sand at the bottom of the fall, and with prayers in their hearts they booted the animals safely over the precipice.

The children and baggage were handed down while the women were helped along the narrow ledge on the canyon wall where Manly "had to creep on hands and knees, or be dashed down fifty feet to certain death" when he coaxed the little mule across the ledge. After reassembling the small train, the families clambered over boulders and down more rock falls. They paused in sadness as they passed the bodies of two of the horses Manly and Rogers were forced to abandon. Near the mouth of the canyon they followed an Indian trail down the alluvial fan and thus did not see the spectacular dry-fall now named for Manly, a fall now obliterated by the Briggs open-pit gold mine.

Manly and Rogers pushed ahead with the oxen across southern Panamint Valley to prepare camp in a deep canyon in the Slate Range. The women came into camp two hours late, and "when they reached the beds they fell at full length on them,

---

[15] Some writers have attributed the naming of Death Valley to Mrs. Brier, but Manly makes it clear that one of these three men named it. We think Manly named Death Valley.

Abigail Arcan and Sarah Bennett were helped around "Ox-Jump Fall" in Redlands Canyon after the men pushed the oxen and mule over the precipice onto a bed of sand below.

saying their feet and limbs ached like the tooth ache.... Their soup was carried to them in bed, and they were covered up as they lay, and slept till morning." Camp was in upper Fish Canyon about two hundred yards northeast of where Manly and Rogers had found the body of their dead companion, Mr. Fish. Manly paid his last respects to his friend and found that although the body was covered only with sagebrush, it "had not been disturbed and looked quite natural." Reverend Brier, with whom Mr. Fish had been traveling when he died a month before, said of the canyon below this camping place:

> The Canyon ... closed up to 20 feet in width, with walls on either side overhanging or perpendicular—A Silent Supulcre.... The place was not only dismal in the extreme, but dangerous. Indians were watching us from the heights of that I was aware, because I saw their fresh tracks in the wet sand.... They could have rolled rocks on us from above & have buried us.[16]

The next day the weary travelers climbed over Manly Pass and descended the Slate Range through the middle fork of Isham Canyon. The difficulty of getting the oxen up the steep hillside to the pass and down the dry-falls in the middle fork of Isham Canyon was responsible for the short drive of only a couple miles covered that day. Manly said, "our oxen would only creep along, picking out the way so as to favor their sore feet."[17] The women and children were also having difficulty with the descent:

> Our road now led down the western slope of the mountain, and loose, hard, broken rocks were harder on the feet of our animals than coming up, and our own moccasins were wearing through.

[16] James Brier, letter JA 76, Jayhawker Collection, Huntington Library, also reprinted in *Escape from Death Valley*, p. 183.

[17] This camp is not mentioned in Manly's book, but it is alluded to in "From Vermont to California." See *Escape from Death Valley*, p. 121.

The cattle needed shoes as well as we. Any one who has never tried it can not imagine how hard it is to walk with tender feet over broken rock.... The sun shone very hot, and with no water we suffered fearfully.

Manly and Rogers hurried the cattle across Searles Valley to a little stream at the foot of Argus Peak where they uncovered the small sack of wheat they had cached on their return trip to Death Valley. Beside the little stream that issued from Providence Spring, in Indian Joe Canyon, the boys slaughtered an ox saving the blood for soup and sewing the hides into moccasins for humans and oxen alike.[18] Behind them the others plodded slowly through the loose sand of Searles Valley with Old Crump, who, bearing his precious load of four children, ground his teeth from lack of food and water. As they trudged across the valley, they could see Searles Lake to the south with the Trona Pinnacles beyond looking like conifer trees in the shimmering heat. Manly and Rogers had regrettably gone to the lake on their first trip out and described it as "strong alkali, red as wine and slippery to the touch."[19]

They crossed Searles Valley not far north of Mr. Isham's shallow grave where the Jayhawkers had buried him under a thin covering of desert sand. Of the five men who died along the "shortcut"— Culverwell, Fish, Isham, Naylor, and

---

[18] This spring and the little stream issuing from it were named Providence Spring by Juliet Brier who camped here a month before the Bennett-Arcan group. While some of the Jayhawkers hunted for water in the Argus Range, Juliet prayed in the shade of the great boulders at Point of Rocks a mile north of Trona. As Juliet prayed for deliverance, Luther Richards brought word that he had found water in today's Indian Joe Canyon located three miles to the north.

[19] The red color was produced by halophilic bacteria that flourishes in salty lakes including the northern part of Great Salt Lake. See *Escape from Death Valley*, note 42.

Robinson—the first three had traveled together from Salt Lake to Death Valley. Their deaths gave mute testimony to the rigors of the trail the families must follow. Naylor died at Mt. Misery in Utah near the beginning of the cutoff.

When the women came into camp about dusk, Manly recalls they "were as usual, and their appearance would remind one quite strongly of half-drowned hens which had not been long out of trouble. Hair snarled, eyes red, nose swollen, and out of fix generally. They did not sleep well so much fatigued [were they], for they said they lived over their hard days in dreams at night."

After spending the night at Providence Spring, the Bennett-Arcan group had to cross the Argus Range and the wide basin of Indian Wells Valley before they could reach the next good water at the foot of the Sierra Nevada. Manly described it by saying,

> There was now before us a particularly bad stretch of the country as it would probably take us four or five days to get over it [Indian Wells Valley], and there was only one water hole in the entire distance. This one was quite salt, so much so that on our return trip the horses refused to drink it, and the little white one died the next day.

The bedraggled caravan worked their way up east Wilson Canyon and camped on a small plateau where they enjoyed a grand panoramic view of the southern Sierra Nevada. Two tall boulders that stood like sentinels at the west end of the plateau provided scant shelter from the chilling night breeze. They descended the western flank of the Argus Range through Deadman Canyon, which was "filled with great boulders, over which it was very difficult to get oxen along." This was the same canyon the Jayhawkers and Brier family had used a month before and the same one Manly and Rogers had traversed on their return to Death Valley.

The next camp was at the "quite salt" water hole three miles north of China Lake in Indian

Wells Valley. Years later Paxton built his ranch here and raised horses whose descendants still roam the Coso and Argus mountains. The families boiled their wheat and ox meat in the salty water, but it did not soften as it did in fresh water. The oxen refused to drink the unhealthy water and wandered about looking for something palatable to chew.

The younger children required constant care from Abigail and Sarah; they all pleaded for water. During the day the babies cried in their cramped pockets, but George and Melissa sometimes walked when the trail was smooth. Now the mothers were plagued by a new torment. "Little Charley Arcane broke out with a bad looking rash all over his body and as he cried most of the time it no doubt smarted and pained him like a mild burn. Neither his mother nor any one else could do anything for him to give him relief." They all suffered with his pitiful crying.

For two days they plodded through the sands of Indian Wells Valley. There was no water for the animals and only salty water for the humans. Fortunately they traveled a trail broken by some of the Jayhawkers and the Brier family who had passed that way. Along with the others, Abigail kept walking mile after mile asking no special favors nor causing undue delays during the forced march.

The pitiful band finally reached the foot of the Sierra Nevada, and for the first time in months they had ample sweet water to drink. From Indian Wells at the foot of Owens Peak, they bore south on an ancient Indian trail. This broad trail was used by Indians who stole horses from the ranchos in the San Fernando and San Joaquin valleys. Some of the horses were herded all the way to Utah for trade; others were driven to Indian villages throughout the desert for food.

The next camp was south of Freeman Junction —the turnoff to Walker Pass. Snow had closed the pass after the vanguard of Death Valley '49ers had been fortunate enough to cross it.[20] As the little band spread their blankets, the wind rose, and the clear desert air grew cold. Even the oxen stood near the fire for warmth. Not far off stood the solitary mass of rocks now called Robbers Roost. Years later Manly said the rocks looked like the great stone chimney of the boiler house at Stanford University; he figured the only students in the area would be lizards. Abigail may have wrapped little Charley in the treasured table cloth she wore around her waist.

By this time all the supplies brought from the Rancho San Francisco had been eaten. For the rest of the trip, only the lean ox meat butchered along the trail would keep them alive. "The meat was tough and stringy as basswood bark, and tasted strongly of bitter sage brush," Manly complained. It was hardly a sustaining diet for a man, much less a woman carrying a growing child within her.

They followed the Indian horse thief trail southeasterly to the unassuming crest of the El Paso Mountains where they could look south over the seemingly interminable Mojave Desert. At their feet was the rugged descent into Last Chance Canyon where they found a small spring of potable water under the steep walls delicately shaded pink, rose, and yellow. But color is the canyon's only soft aspect. The families descended a steep hillside into the rugged canyon bottom where they found the small spring but no grass for the cattle. Manly described their descent:

---

[20] The Georgia contingent, who had previously been travel-ing with the Brier family, left their remaining oxen with the Briers and crossed Towne Pass while the Jayhawkers were burning their wagons at McLean Spring. About 20 of these men crossed Walker Pass before a snowstorm closed it, and they arrived in emaciated condition at the Mariposa diggings. See *Death Valley in '49*, pp. 373-376 and George W. B. Evans, *Mexican Gold Trail* (Huntington Library, 1945, San Marino, CA), pp. 254 & 259.

The hill we had just come down was very rough and rocky and our progress very slow, every step made in a selected spot. We could not stop here to kill an ox and let the remainder of them starve, but must push on to where the living ones could get a little food.... One of the women held up her foot and the sole was bare and blistered. She said they ached like a toothache. The women had left their combs in the wagons, and their hair was getting seriously tangled. Their dresses were getting worn off pretty nearly to their knees.... They were in a sad condition so far as toilet and raiment were concerned.

Next morning they limped down the canyon, suffering from stiff joints and tender feet. Their goal was a small spring about 12 miles away, now called Desert Spring. But they did not reach it. Dusk descended as they emerged from Last Chance Canyon onto the broad expanse of the Mojave Desert. They camped beside a small playa two miles southwest of the canyon mouth, and during the night a winter storm blew in. Manly recalled, "We laid down as close as pigs in cold weather, and covered up as best we could, but did not keep dry, and morning found us wet to the skin, cold and shivering...the tracks of our nearly bare feet could be plainly seen in the snow which lay like a blanket awhile over the ground, about two inches deep."

After the sun melted the snow, they pushed on the few miles to the little spring, which they found surrounded by a willow corral. Indians had woven the willows to create a fence to contain the horses they stole from the ranchos in the coastal regions.

Abigail soothed little Charley's burning rash with the cool spring water, a rash that may have been a symptom of malnutrition or possibly an allergic reaction to Old Crump. The men dried strips of stringy meat over the fire and made new moccasins from the hide of a freshly slaughtered ox while the women rested and tended their battered feet and the ailing children.[21]

The next water source was two days away across the Mojave Desert in shallow rainwater holes near Rosamond [Dry] Lake northeast of today's Palmdale. Today, in startling contrast to the past, part of their route is covered with alfalfa fields watered from deep wells near California City. But in 1850, the Bennett and Arcan families followed a dry trail littered with the bones of horses and cattle that had died of thirst before they reached the spring at the willow corral. The bones were from some of the animals stolen from the Rancho San Francisco, a favorite raiding spot for Indian horse thieves.

The trail itself was hard-packed earth, but if the little one-eyed mule stepped to the side, she would sink "six inches deep into the soft sand, and the labor of walking...[was] immense." Manly continued, "I stepped out to examine the peculiar soil and found it finer than superfine flour."[22] Only stunted sage brush and a few "cabbage trees," as Manly called the Joshua trees, broke the barren monotony of the Mojave landscape.

Manly and Rogers hurried the cattle forward to make camp at the rainwater holes located on what is now Edwards Air Force Base where the shuttles land after their missions in space. The water in these depressions was only about an inch deep, and the same condition exists today after a desert rain. The families came along more slowly with Old Crump carrying the children. John Arcan often carried Charley because Charley

---

[21] A California Historical monument stands at the site where tamarisk have replaced the willows; the spring is now dry. It is 0.9 mile south of the intersection of Valley and Papas roads on private land.

[22] In *From Vermont to California* Manly says, "the ground was very soft and light as snuff." The change from snuff to flour is one of several that indicate a woman helped Manly write *Death Valley in '49*.

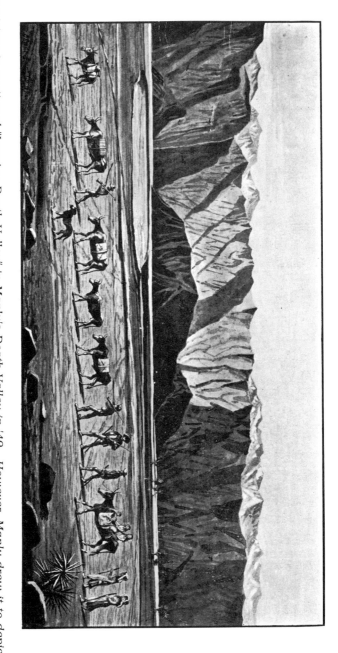

This picture is captioned "Leaving Death Valley" in Manly's Death Valley in '49. However, Manly drew it to depict a scene later in the journey, probably crossing the Mojave Desert. Note that only five of the original eleven oxen remain. Arcan has thrown away his gun, the women's dresses are worn off almost to their knees, and there are Joshua trees in the background, a species not native to Death Valley.

"seemed to grow worse rather than better. His whole body was red as fire, and he screamed with the pain and torment of the severe itching. Nothing could be done to relieve him, and if his strength lasted till we could get better air, water and food he might recover, but his chances were very poor." It is difficult to imagine the anxiety and frustration the Arcans felt at being unable to ease his pain and soothe his constant crying. But sickness and death were common experiences during the westward migration. Accidents and illness "were continual shadows upon the pioneer's lives. But for the women, those shadows were intensified by the twin circumstances of pregnancy and birth."[23]

From the rainwater holes they continued south toward a depression in the San Gabriel Mountains now called Soledad Pass. They expected to reach some springs at the base of the mountains by nightfall, but again they fell short of their goal.

> The soil was of the finest dust with no grit in it, and not long before a light shower had fallen, making it very soft and hard to get along in with the moccasins. The women had to stop to rest frequently, so our progress was very slow. Rogers and I had feet about as hard as those of the oxen, so we removed our moccasins and went barefoot, finding we could get along much easier in that way, but the others had such tender feet they could not endure the rough contact with the brush and mud. Only a few miles had been made before the women were so completely tired out that we had to stop and eat our little bit of dried meat and wait till morning.

The night was cool with breezes off the snow in the San Gabriel Mountains as the exhausted emigrants were forced to make a dry camp near today's Lancaster. Stalks from the dead cabbage trees provided a blazing campfire, but a fire was their only comfort. The cattle ground their teeth but had no cud to chew. Little Charley cried and

---

[23] Lillian Schlissel, p. 58. (*See note 2.*)

fretted with his burning rash. The women had new pains from back-sliding with each step on the slippery mud. They were out of water and had the added disappointment of not reaching their intended goal.

> For breakfast in the morning we had only dried meat roasted before the fire, without water, and when we started each one put a piece in his or her pocket to chew on during the day as we walked along.

Finally they reached "standing water in several large holes." This campsite, now called Barrel Springs four miles southeast of Palmdale, was frequented by Indian raiders and the *Californios* who chased them into the desert in a futile attempt to retrieve their stolen livestock.

The next day the tattered band approached Soledad Pass, but the sun had softened the snow and they could not proceed. Another ox was killed and its flesh dried over a juniper fire. The men made several small fires to heat the ground upon which they spread the blankets so the families might benefit from the warmed earth underneath.

They started very early the next morning to take advantage of the frozen, crusted snow, and as they neared the summit of the pass, the weary travelers looked back over the country they had traversed the last twenty days. They had struggled over 200 miles since abandoning their wagons. In the distant northeast, snowy Telescope Peak towered over the nearer ranges and wide plains over which they had struggled.[24] This majestic peak marked the spot where the two families had worried and waited for rescue, and now it stood as a monument over the grave of Captain Culverwell. At their feet, the Mojave

---

[24] Today Telescope Peak is often obscured by smog, but on a clear winter day, early in the morning, the majestic snow-clad peak can be seen from the vista point on the freeway that crosses Soledad Pass. The peak is also visible from the hill a quarter mile north of Barrel Spring.

Desert stretched north to the El Paso Mountains, a streak of hazy blue in the distance.

Their route over the snow-covered pass was six miles of slippery, glaring white before they descended to the brush-clogged slopes of Soledad Canyon. But soon the families came to the embodiment of their fondest hopes, the promise that kept them going, the lure held in front of them for so long— "blessed water! There it danced and jumped over the rocks singing the merriest song one ever heard." They camped at once. This small brook, two miles southwest of Acton, surfaces in Thousand Trails Recreation Park and flows for a short distance before sinking underground only to reappear again and again in its descent.

The famished group needed food, so Manly took the mule and hunted for game. As dusk settled, he shot a yearling cow and loaded the mule with "the hind quarter skinned out, and all the fat" he could find. It was after midnight when Manly and the heavily laden little mule finally stumbled into camp with their precious load. The families were roused from their beds, and soon chunks of fresh, fat beef were roasting over the fire. "They ate the delicate morsels with a relish and, most of all, praised the sweet fat."

However, their over indulgence brought grief the next day. An early camp was hastily made when Sarah Bennett was "suddenly taken sick with severe pain and vomiting." Their digestive systems could not tolerate the rich, fat meat. This camp, under a great live-oak tree, was an overwhelming contrast to what they had known for months. The ground was covered with a deep bed of dry leaves overlooking a lush, green meadow. After the little band rested, bathed, washed clothes, and ate some more, they gave thanks for their deliverance from the Great American Desert.

Their route down Soledad Canyon followed the Jayhawkers' trail (which in turn followed Manly and Rogers' first trail), but the blessed stream exacted a price from the weary pioneers. The thick brush and brambles forced them to wade through the stream, and "sometimes the women fell down, for a rawhide moccasin soaked soft in water was not a very comfortable or convenient shoe." What an understatement! Walking on slippery rocks with wet moccasins was like crossing a stream on a greased pole. After many dunkings, the women gave out, and another camp was made. The women stood before the fire in their soaked and tattered dresses "turning round and round to get warm and dry." Manly provided a vivid description:

> Someone remarked that they resembled geese hanging before the fire to roast, as they slowly revolved, and it was all owing to their fatigue that the suggestor did not receive merited punishment then and there at their hands. As they got a little dry and comfortable they remarked that even the excess of water like this was better than the desert where there was none at all, and as to their looks, there were no society people about to point their fingers at them, and when they reached a settled country they hoped to have a chance to change their clothes, and get two dresses apiece, and that these would be long enough to hide their knees which these poor tatters quite failed to do. One remarked that she was sure she had been down in the brook a dozen times and that she did not consider cold water baths so frequently repeated were good for the health.

Two days later, on March 7, the families arrived at the *hacienda* of the Rancho San Francisco where they conversed in sign language and the few Spanish words Manly had learned when he bought supplies there almost six weeks earlier. The destitute pioneers were fed and cared for by the Del Valle family with "genuine sympathy and hospitality on their part, and none of us ever forgot it."

With profuse thanks for leading his family to safety, John Arcan gave a light gold ring to Manly and to John Rogers a silver watch wishing he had more to share with them. Each family had two remaining oxen plus Bennett's faithful Old Crump who had carried his precious burden with stately dignity.[25] John Arcan traded his oxen for assistance over the mountains to the ocean port of San Pedro where he booked passage for his family to San Francisco.[26]

The Arcans may have been advised that San Francisco was not a fit place for a destitute family or, since they had no money, they may not have been able to convince the captain to take them that far. In either case, the Arcans settled in the small sea-side village of Santa Cruz where there were only about 20 families. Almost everything they brought from the east was lost—two wagons, their household goods and tools of trade, all the oxen, and all of their money. Only Abigail's tablecloth remained. While John went to the gold fields, Abigail, with little Charley, stayed in Santa Cruz to await the arrival of her baby.

Four months after the Arcans' exodus from the desert, baby Julia was born. It is doubtful John returned from his search for gold in time to help Abigail through her ordeal. As was the case with so many pioneer women, she faced the trauma of childbirth without friends or relatives in a strange country. Their baby was named in honor of

---

[25] After the Bennett family arrived at the gold fields, a farmer who lived near French Camp bought Old Crump. When Manly saw him in 1856, he was "fat and sleek," grazing in a lush pasture. His owner would neither sell nor work him in honor of his valorous part in the rescue from Death Valley.

[26] Manly, Rogers, and the Bennetts continued to Los Angeles where friends, who had followed Captain Hunt down the Spanish Trail, were waiting. Manly remained in Los Angeles and worked for the Brier family until he earned enough money to travel north with the little one-eyed mule. The Bennetts procured a wagon, and with the others, including John Rogers, they made their way up the coast to San Jose and east to the gold fields.

another brave and gentle pioneer who also experienced the travails of the desert trek—Juliet Brier (Julia to her friends).[27] Her middle initial may have stood for Sarah in honor of Sarah Bennett. Julia's death 19 days after her birth placed an additional burden of grief upon the already stricken family. Julia was the first person to be buried in the newly created Evergreen Cemetery in Santa Cruz.[28]

Why do we extend the dubious honor of causing Julia's death to the valley of that name? The nourishment needed by Abigail and her unborn daughter was not to be found in that barren land. The final spoonfuls of rice and tea had been given to Manly and Rogers to nourish them during their rescue mission; everything left was given to the four young children, especially little Martha Bennett who teetered on the verge of death. A skinny ox and perhaps a duck or goose from the salty lake near Eagle Borax Spring were the only sources of sustenance. There were no vegetables or fruits or grains or milk. Beans from the mesquite trees that grew around the springs in Death Valley ripened in July and had been collected by the Indians or eaten by rodents, and the nutritious pinyon nuts were high in the mountains covered with snow. All the food prepared for their arduous ten-month trek from Illinois had been consumed by the time they entered the desolate, forbidding valley of salt and sand.

After John returned to Santa Cruz from the gold fields, the Arcans made a name for themselves and became what some people termed well-to-do. John bought property at the corner of what is now Pacific and Soquel Avenues, then called the Arcan block. He probably used the gold he had mined for payment, or he may have used

---

[27] Personal communication with E. B. MacBrair-Koller, Berkeley, California, historian for the Brier family.

[28] *Santa Cruz Sentinel*, April 4, 1978.

credit based on his Masonic ties. He was a charter member of the Santa Cruz Masonic Lodge, which was established in 1853.

As years passed, two more daughters were born to the Arcans. Julia Madeline was born in early 1861 when Abigail was 44. Madeline required a great deal of care because she was retarded. Abigail was listed in the 1880 census as a nurse, possibly because of the extensive care Madeline required.[29] Madeline died at the age of 26 in the spring of 1887.

Abigail Carolyn (Abby) was born about a year after Madeline. Her mother was at the advanced age of 45, late in life in the 1800s for a safe pregnancy. Carolyn married John A. Flores, a butcher, in 1891 when she was 30 years old. Since this was rather late in life for marriage in those days, she may have remained unmarried to help her mother care for Madeline. Five years after her marriage, John Flores died in an accident, and Abby married his brother. She bore three daughters, but only one survived her—Ella (Mrs. Fred P.) Harder—who also resided in Santa Cruz most of her life. Abby was bed-ridden and unable to speak for five years before her death in 1918.

It is not clear in what year the Arcans built their home at the corner of Arcan Street (now called Soquel Avenue) and Pacific Avenue, but it was probably in 1854. The old Bank of America building now stands on the Arcan home site. The clapboard house was an eastern design with a peaked gable roof, rows of small-paned windows

---

[29] One of the problems researchers face is the accuracy of the materials they use. Our first edition stated that Abigail was 38 years old when Madeline was born based on the 1880 census, which was apparently wrong. The 1870 census and Abigail's obituary (*Santa Cruz Daily Sentinel*, February 25, 1891) agree on her age; making her 44 when Madeline was born. There is also a conflict in the data for the birth year of daughter Abigail Carolyn.

upstairs and down, and a porch across the front. A wall down the middle of the long rectangular house separated the living quarters from John's gunsmith shop. The Masonic Lodge met upstairs from 1855 to 1868. In the late 1870s, the sturdy structure was moved around the corner to face Soquel Avenue. About this time Abigail sold the building, which was later used as a restaurant and then a grocery store.

John had been a leader in his community for almost 20 years when he died of apoplexy in 1869 on September 15, while he worked in his garden. His obituary referred to John as "a man of genial, complaisant nature, happy temperament, agreeable conversations—always having a compliment and kind word for everyone, thus acquiring many friends and admirers." Eighty-two Masons attended his funeral at the Methodist Church, and he was buried near his baby daughter Julia in Evergreen Cemetery. He left Abigail with two young daughters to care for.

Charley was 21 when his father died, and he and his young family apparently lived with Abigail, Madeline, and Abby in the home that John had built. Charley was nineteen when he married Josephine Chaurett who gave birth to five children during the next ten years. He plied many trades during his life in Santa Cruz including machinist, teamster, and later, a bar owner on Pacific Avenue.

After Josephine's death, Charley married Etta Berry Emery in 1889. During his later years, Charley played a small saxhorn in the Hastings Band, the first of the Santa Cruz beach bands. They clothed themselves in discarded Civil War uniforms and played for special gatherings. In 1907 Charley died of rheumatism at 59 years of age.

Abigail gave Etta her treasured tablecloth, the one she wore around her waist when leaving Death Valley, the only surviving article from their two wagon-loads of goods.

A magazine article by Mr. K. Kevil for "News and Notes from the Santa Cruz Historical Society," February 1960, described Abigail's tablecloth saying the cloth was "71 inches wide and 72 inches long. It was cut from a bolt of cloth and the ends have hand sewn hems, with stitches that are unbelievably fine. It is of the delicate Dicer pattern with half-inch squares of slightly contrasting color." Abigail wove the bolt of linen on a hand loom and the pattern was a popular one before mechanical looms became common. use.

Etta said Abigail treasured the tablecloth and used it only for very special occasions. In 1939, at 84 years of age, Etta said the cloth was now a rather dull white, whereas it had been an attractive cream color. It was exhibited at Furnace Creek Inn in 1942 and again in 1949 during the Centennial Gold Rush Celebration in Death Valley.

Abigail was as elusive in death as she was in life. On February 25, 1891, *The Santa Cruz Daily Sentinel*, carried her brief obituary: "ARCAN—In this city, Feb. 24th, Mrs. Abigail H. Arcan, a native of Massachusetts, aged 74 years." There is no known record of her funeral or burial, although an unmarked plot spans the distance between John's and baby Julia's grave stones. No monument or other sign indicates she is buried there.

Abigail's strength, stamina, and determination were exceptional by today's standards but were typical of the pioneer women who wove the fabric of our western history. She deserves to stand with William Lewis Manly, John Haney Rogers, and Juliet Brier as a prominent heroine of Death Valley in 1849.

Abigail carried her unborn child, baby Julia, out of Death Valley only to lose her after

A little time on earth she spent
'Till God for her his angel sent.

FOLLOWING THE BENNETT-ARCAN ROUTE BY CAR

(Bold letters in text refer to locations on map, page 26.)

You may start anywhere along the route, but the farthest east location for a car is Indian Springs on highway 395 north of Las Vegas. (**A**) The wagons followed a route similar to the current highway west to Point of Rocks beyond which they overlooked the wide Amargosa Valley. A dirt road crosses the valley and a small gap in the hills ahead, where, on the other side, is the eastern-most outpost of Death Valley National Park—Devils Hole in Ash Meadows northeast of Death Valley Junction. (**B**)

Nusbaumer recorded in his diary that as they entered Ash Meadows from the east, "to the right is a hole in the rocks [Devils Hole], which contains magnificent warm water and in which Hadapp and I enjoyed an extremely refreshing bath. The temperature of the water is about 75-79° F and the saline cavity itself presents a magical appearance."

To the southwest of Devils Hole, you see trees about a mile away at Collins Spring where the Bennett-Arcan train of seven wagons found grass, wood, and good water for their camp. This spring is not named on the USGS quadrangle map.

Farther to the west, after crossing the "horrible alkali marshes," as Nusbaumer described Carson Slough in the bottom of Ash Meadows, they ascended the Funeral Range about where highway 190 heads west toward Death Valley. The small caravan spent Christmas eve about 5 miles west of Death Valley Junction.

After the wagon train crossed the pass and descended Furnace Creek Wash, they camped a few days at Travertine Springs about 2 miles east of Furnace Creek Inn. (**C**) In the center of the

Inn's gravel parking lot, a large boulder with several metates ground into it is all that remains of the Indian village that once occupied this site. John Rogers said, "We found a big Indian camp. Their fires were still burning and the Indians gone, except an old man who was blind. He was crawling around on the ground. He had a little willow basket full of muddy water and had a sharp stick which he was using in digging up roots."

From here, look west and imagine the Panamint Range covered with snow barring your passage west. Some of the emigrants thought they were facing the great Sierra Nevada, and if so, Walker Pass would be to the south. As you look south down Death Valley, you can see a notch in the range, a possible way across the mountain. As you drive south on the paved road, you parallel the route the dry, creaking Bennett-Arcan wagons took along the alluvial fan toward that notch in late December, 1849. Like the '49ers, you are following an Indian trail.

Near where the west-side road crosses Devil's Golf Course, the wagons crossed the salty white expanse. When you reach the west side of the valley, imagine the caravan turning south to parallel the current west-side road on the smoothest and least boulder-strewn part of the alluvial fans at the edge of the salt pan. At Tule Spring, Nusbaumer and his companion Hadapp found their first "warm sweet spring" of water since leaving Travertine Springs two days before. They boiled four pots of coffee to combat the thirst from drinking the blood of a sick ox that had been abandoned.

The Bennett-Arcan families stopped at Eagle Borax Spring where the four teamsters left the two families and followed the Jayhawkers over Towne Pass, far to the north (see map page 25).

About 9 $^1/2$ miles south of Eagle Borax Spring (about 100 yards southeast of bench mark (BM) - 246 on the Bennett Well quadrangle map) they came to what we judge was the location of Manly's little sulphur water well. In later years it was the site of Mesquite Well, the last stop in Death Valley where teamsters drew fresh water for the 20-mule teams that pulled the loaded borax wagons to Daggett. There is no sign of water now.

After attempting to get their wagons up the Warm Spring fan over the Pleistocene desert pavement (a smoother route than the current roads), the two families returned first to the little sulphur water well, and then to Eagle Borax Spring to wait for Manly and Rogers' return with provisions and horses. The "long camp," where the families waited for Manly and Rogers, was located at two places—first at Eagle Borax Spring, then 2.5 miles south at Bennetts Well where abundant bunch grass grew and where they dug for better water. (**D**)

From Bennetts Well, the notch in the range —the upper part of Galena Canyon—appears to be the shortest route over the mountain. After Manly and Rogers' returned, the two families packed up and traveled south 4 or 5 miles when the oxen started their bucking spree.

Instead of continuing over the course Manly and Rogers had used (Warm Spring Canyon), they headed cross-country toward the gap, which we call Galena Gap. After ascending the main branch of Galena Canyon and crossing the gap, they dropped into upper Warm Spring Canyon, crossed a narrow part of Butte Valley, and ascended the slope to Arrastre Spring. (**E**)

As you drive up the mine road to Galena Canyon, you can see why Bennett and Arcan did not take their wagons up this fan; it is far too rough. But when on foot, the nearness of Galena Gap was too tempting to resist. A cable usually blocks the road into the canyon, but you can walk up the road and as far into the canyon as you wish. The spring is about a mile and a half up-canyon from the talc mines.

From the upper entrance of Warm Spring Canyon, you can see Arrastre Spring on the hillside to the west. Depending on the condition of the road in Butte Valley, you can parallel the families' route as they skirted southward along the west side of Butte Valley. The road to Redlands Canyon passes south of Striped Butte, but the families cut north of the butte and camped at Redlands Spring deep in Redlands Canyon. (**F**) The road terminates about three miles from the spring.

Ask the Park Service about road conditions in Goler Wash before attempting to drive it. When it isn't washed out, it usually requires a 4-wheel drive vehicle. If you can get down Goler Wash (south out of Butte Valley), turn north in Panamint Valley to Redlands Canyon to see where the families exited the Panamint Range. Looking south of west, you see Manly Pass as the low place in the Slate Range, the only logical place to cross. Fish Canyon, the canyon the families ascended, penetrates the northeastern side of the pass.

If you can't drive down Goler Wash, backtrack to Towne Pass, go south in Panamint Valley to the site of Ballarat and further south to Redlands Canyon, which is the big canyon just before you circle the toe of Manly Peak and the site of the Briggs open-pit gold mine. Or by-pass Ballarat and pick up the trail in Searles Valley north of Trona.

Near Valley Wells in Searles Valley, look northeast, back to Manly Pass where the families came down Isham Canyon. Walk out through the brush to get a feel for the decomposed granite sand the families trudged through.

To the west is Wilson Canyon through which they climbed the Argus Range. Pioneer Point, just north of Trona, is the rocky outcrop where Mrs. Brier was praying when Deacon Richards came with shouts that he had found water. (**G**) Mrs. Brier's Providence Spring is in Indian Joe Canyon just north of Wilson Canyon. This is the spring

Manly and Rogers missed when they went for supplies because they headed due west from the northern edge of Searles Lake. A day later they learned the location of Providence Spring from the Jayhawkers encamped at Indian Wells Spring at the toe of Owens Peak. On their return trip to Death Valley the boys buried a bag of wheat in Indian Joe Canyon. From Trona, head southwest to Ridgecrest.

As you drive west from Ridgecrest toward highway 14, you have the same view of the Sierra Nevada as did the families when they crossed Indian Wells Valley. Near highway 14 you cross over the '49ers' trail where they trudged southwest to Indian Wells Spring at today's Homestead. (**H**)

Turn south on highway 14 to Homestead (about 1.7 miles). Indian Wells Spring issues from an earthquake fault behind the buildings. From here to Freeman Junction, the turnoff to Walker Pass, the families paralleled the highway about where the Los Angeles aqueduct was later built further up the hill. When Manly and Rogers came this way, they could see that snow prevented passage over Walker Pass, so they continued south.

Southwest of Freeman Junction you see the butte called Robbers Roost that Manly described as looking like "the great stone chimney of the boiler house at Stanford University." The families camped within sight of this natural monument.

Highway 14 enters Redrock Canyon, but the small caravan did not go that way. They followed the well-worn Indian trail that led to the freshwater springs in Last Chance Canyon. You can drive several dirt roads to the low crest overlooking the depths of the canyon and across the vast Mojave Desert to the south. With a rugged vehicle, you *may* be able to negotiate part of the canyon from the Redrock-Randsburg road.

After driving through Redrock Canyon, you are about 6 miles from Desert Spring (Manly's willow corral) where a California Historical monument says: "This spring was [on] an old Indian horse thief trail and later (1834) Joe Walker Trail. The famished Manly-Jayhawk Death Valley parties (1849-50) were revived here after coming from Indian Wells through Last Chance Canyon. This was also a station on the Nadeau Borax Freight Road." (**I**)

To find Desert Spring, take Neuralia Road due south at the intersection of highway 14 and the road to Randsburg. Go one mile south, and after crossing the railroad tracks, turn northeast 1.3 mile to the site of Cantil. Turn east on Valley Road 1 mile to Pappas Road and south on Pappas for half a mile, passing a couple of houses. You can see the tamarisk trees at Desert Spring, which is on private property, about a fourth mile west of the second house. Just south of the house, a small dirt road leads to the site of the spring. Ask permission from the property owners before going into the spring site.

If you follow Neuralia Road south, you are close to the route of the Indian horse-thief trail, which the families followed. At California City, turn west on the Randsburg-Mojave Road and return to Highway 14.

At Rosamond, enter Edwards Air Force Base and follow Rosamond Boulevard east about 8^1/2 miles. The road crosses the families' trail to the rainwater holes that lay between Rosamond and Buckhorn Dry Lakes about 2 miles south of the road.

Return to the freeway or to the old highway (Sierra) from Rosamond to Palmdale and turn east on Highway 138 to Pearland. Stay south on 47th Street instead of turning east with Highway 138. Go about 2 miles south and turn northwest (right) on Barrel Springs Road. Go about 2 miles to Barrel Springs nestled in the San Andreas Fault. A park not far from the springs. (**J**)

If the day is clear and if Telescope Peak is topped with snow, you can see it far to the north from the hill one quarter mile north of Barrel Spring. You can also see it from the view point on the freeway over Soledad Pass.

Take the old highway (Pearblossom leads right into it) over Soledad Pass to the Thousand Trails Recreation Park where the families found the bubbling spring. From here the road follows the brushy canyon where the families slipped and slid down the little stream.

Cross under Interstate 5 to Castaic Junction. Look south across the Santa Clara River to the site of the ranch house of the San Francisco Rancho on the hill overlooking the river. (**K**) The remains of the adobe ranch house have been bull-dozed away, but you may see horses grazing on the hill where they grazed 150 years ago.

To follow the route on foot, consult *Escape from Death Valley*.

Index

Arcan (Arcane), family, 3, 5,
 6, 10, 12, 34, 41-45
Arcan,
 Abigail, 5, 6, 7, 8, 10,
  12-14, 19, 21-23, 25,
  28, 32-33, 42-45
 Abigail (Abby) Carolyn,
  43
 Charley (Charlie), 5, 10,
  22, 32-37, 41, 44
 John, 10, 21, 39, 40, 41,
  44
 Julia, 6. 9, 10, 42, 45
 Julia Madeline, 43
 Etta, 44, 45
 See also Bennett-Arcan
  party/route
Arcan home, 43-44
Argus Range, 17, 31, 50
Arrastre Spring, 25, 49
Ash Meadows, 47
Barney Ward, 11
Barrel Springs, 38, 52
Beaver Dam Wash, 12,
Bennett-Arcan party, 14-
 16, 17, 22
Bennett-Arcan route, 23-40
Bennett family, 12, 15, 41
 Martha, 21, 42
 Sarah, 13, 22, 39
 See also Bennett-Arcan
  party/route
Bennetts Well, 18, 21, 48
Brier family, 12
 James Welch, 29
 Juliet, 15, 16
Briggs Gold Mine,
Butte Valley, 24, 47
Christmas, 15-16
Cuff, 18, 21, 22
Culverwell, Captain, 10,
 15, 17, 19, 21, 23, 30
Deadman Canyon, 31
Death Valley, 5, 10, 17, 25,
 47
Death Valley Junction, 15,
 47
Desert Spring, 34, 50, 51
Devils Hole, 47

Eagle Borax Spring, 17,
 19, 48, 48
Earhart, 15, 17, 19
El Paso Mountains, 33,
 51
Fish Canyon, 29, 48
Fish, Father, 15, 20, 29
Fremont's map, 11
Furnace Creek Wash, 16,
 46
Galena Canyon, 25, 48
Hadapp, 15, 19, 46
Horse thief trail, 32, 33,
 35, 36
Hunt, Jefferson, 11, 12
Indian trail, 17
Indian Springs, 46
Indian Wells Valley, 31,
 32, 50
Indians, 17, 21
Isham Canyon, 29, 49
Isham, 15, 20, 29, 33
Jayhawkers, 12, 13, 16,
 20, 30, 32, 39, 47, 49
Last Chance Canyon, 33-
 34
Manly, William Lewis, 12,
 18, 19, 20, 21, 26, 30,
 41
Manly Pass, 27
McLean Spring, 16
Mesquite Well, 18, 21, 48
Mississippi Boys, 12, 15
Mojave Desert, 35-38, 51
Nusbaumer, Louis, 15,
 19
Old Crump, 22, 30, 35,
 40, 41
One-eyed mule, 21, 22
Panamint Range, 17, 18,
 20, 21, 25, 49
Panamint Valley, 27, 49
Paxton Ranch, 31
Providence Spring, 30,
 31, 49
Pueblo de Los Angeles,
 19, 39
Rancho San Francisco,
 20, 40, 52

Redlands Canyon, 21, 26, 26, 27, 28, 49
Rogers, John Haney, 13, 18, 19, 20, 21, 24, 27, 30, 41

San Gabriel Mountains, 20, 37
San Francisco Rancho, 20, *14*, 41, 52
Santa Cruz, 5-7, 41, 42, 43
Schlögel, 15, 17, 19
Searles Valley, 20, 30, 49
Slate Range, 20, 27, 29
Soledad Canyon, 20, 39, 52
Soledad Pass, 20, 37, 39, 52
Sulphur water hole, 18, 21, 48
Tablecloth, 23, 41, 44, 45
Teamsters, 18
Telescope Peak, 38
Travertine Springs, 15, 16, 17, 46
Wade family, 13, 15, 17 19
Walker Pass, 20, 32, 50
Ward, Barney, 11
Warm Spring Canyon, 18, 49
Wilson Canyon, 31, 49